A Kid's Guide to Drawing the Countries of the World™

How to Draw

South Africa's

Sights and Symbols

Melody S. Mis

The Rosen Publishing Group's

PowerKids Press™

New York

To Jack, Nona, and John Rogers

Published in 2004 by The Rosen Publishing Group, Inc.
29 East 21st Street, New York, NY 10010

First Edition

Editor: Jannell Khu
Book Design: Kim Sonsky
Layout Design: Michael de Guzman

Illustration Credits: Cover and inside by Mike Donnellan.
Photo Credits: Cover and title page (hand) by Arlan Dean; Cover (flower), p. 22 © Charles & Josette Lenars/CORBIS; pp. 5, 10, 40, 42 © Charles O'Rear/CORBIS; p. 9 © David Turnley/CORBIS; p. 12 courtesy of Diamond Bozas; p. 13 © Durban Art Gallery; p. 18 © Eric and David Hosking/CORBIS; p. 20 © Michael & Patricia Fogden/CORBIS; p. 26 © AFP/CORBIS; p. 28 © Mark A. Johnson/CORBIS; p. 30 © Earl & Nazima Kowall/CORBIS; p. 32 © Jan Butchofsky-Houser/CORBIS; p. 36 © Stuart Westmorland/CORBIS.

Manufactured in the United States of America

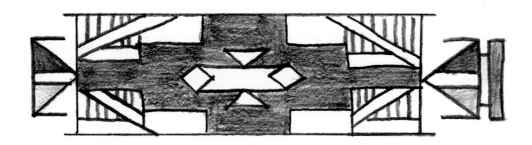

CONTENTS

Let's Draw South Africa

Two or three million years ago, prehistoric people called *Australopithecus africanus* lived in South Africa. Prehistoric people changed over thousands of years and became more like modern men. They learned how to make tools, to trade goods, and to develop their own cultures. Two of the earliest cultures in South Africa were the San and the Khoikhoi. They hunted, gathered food, and raised cattle. Eventually, the San and the Khoikhoi were joined by other groups of people who moved from central and western Africa. The people from these early cultures in South Africa are the ancestors of the country's black population today.

In 1652, people from the Netherlands settled on the Cape of Good Hope to provide supplies for Dutch merchant ships. More people arrived from the Netherlands to farm the land. These farmers were called Boers, which means "farmers" in Dutch. In 1820, the British established colonies on the Cape and became more powerful than the Boers. The Boers did not like British rule, so they moved into the interior of South Africa. The Boers fought and defeated the

During the mid-fifteenth century, Portuguese sailors discovered the southern tip of South Africa, which would later become the Cape of Good Hope. This is a view of the Cape of Good Hope, which is surrounded by the Atlantic Ocean.

black groups that lived in the interior. The Boers then set up their own republics on tribal lands. When diamonds and gold were discovered in South Africa during the nineteenth century, the British and the Boers fought over the rich lands. The British defeated the Boers and formed the Union of South Africa. During British rule, the white minority held most of the political power. Blacks had very little voice in the government that ruled them.

In 1948, D. F. Malan became prime minister of South Africa and introduced apartheid. Apartheid is unfair racial segregation against nonwhite people. Segregation is the separation of different races of people based on their color. Nonwhite people were forced to attend different schools than those attended by whites, and to work where the government placed them. Black people had to live in poor areas and were not allowed to vote. After South Africa gained independence from Britain in 1961, the African National Congress (ANC) led demonstrations over unfair treatment of blacks. Nelson Mandela, leader of the ANC, was sentenced to life in prison. Many other blacks were imprisoned, tortured, or killed, which angered the rest of the world. Some countries stopped trading with South Africa, but the government would not change its apartheid laws. Finally, in 1990, South Africa's president, F. W. de Klerk, freed Mandela, put an end to apartheid, and set up a democratic government in South Africa. In this book, you will learn more about South Africa and how to draw some of the country's sights and symbols. Directions are under each step. New steps are shown in red. You will need the following supplies to draw South Africa's sights and symbols:

- A sketch pad
- An eraser
- A number 2 pencil
- A pencil sharpener

These are some of the shapes and drawing terms you need to know to draw South Africa's sights and symbols:

—— Horizontal line

⁓⁓⁓ Squiggle

⬭ Oval

▱ Trapezoid

▭ Rectangle

△ Triangle

▓ Shading

| Vertical line

∿ Wavy line

More About South Africa

South Africa was nicknamed the Rainbow Nation, after South African archbishop Desmond Tutu described his people as the "rainbow people of God." The name reflects the different colors and cultures of its population. Tutu won the Nobel Peace Prize in 1984 for his work to make sure all South Africans were treated equally.

South Africa is home to more than 43 million people. The black cultures, including the Zulu, Xhosa, Ndebele, and Sesotho, make up about 77 percent of the population. Approximately 11 percent of the population are white, with the majority being Afrikaners. Afrikaners are descendants of the Dutch, French, and German settlers. The rest of the population is made up of people of color and Asians. Many Asians are descendants of the Chinese and Indian laborers who were forced to work on South African sugar farms and in the gold mines.

South Africa does not have one national language. Instead, it has 11 official languages, including Afrikaans, which is a mixture of Dutch and other

This is Archbishop Desmond Tutu during a church service. An archbishop is a high-ranking church official.

9

European languages. Other languages spoken in South Africa include Ndebele, Sesotho, Xhosa, Zulu, and English.

Johannesburg is South Africa's largest and most-populated city, with more than 5.7 million people. Johannesburg was founded on the site of the world's largest gold field. South Africa has three capitals including Cape Town, which is the second-most-populated city with more than two million residents. Pretoria and Bloemfontein are the country's other capitals. The nation's third-most-populated city is Durban, an important port on the Indian Ocean. It has more than 1.3 million people.

South Africa originally had an agricultural economy based on corn, sugarcane, and cattle. These products, along with tobacco, wheat, and fruit, are still grown in South Africa. The nation's economy changed with the discovery of diamonds, gold, and coal. Today South Africa is the world's largest producer of gold and its fifth-largest diamond producer. South Africa's main industries are steel, processed food, chemicals, and textiles.

In little more than a century, Johannesburg has grown from a small mining camp to the most-populated city in South Africa. This is a night-time view of Johannesburg.

The Artist Diamond Bozas

Diamond Bozas is an important and talented South African artist. He is known for his drawings as well as for his watercolors and oil paintings. Bozas is also recognized internationally for his flower arrangements and has been a judge at flower-arranging contests.

Diamond Bozas

Bozas was born in 1923 and attended high school in Eshowe, which is located in an area in Zululand. This area is in the northeastern province of Natal, South Africa. From 1955 to 1960, Bozas studied at the Chelsea School of Art in London, England. After he returned to South Africa, Bozas founded the Zululand Society of Arts and the Vukani Museum in Eshowe. The Vukani Museum has one of the world's best collections of Zulu art.

Today Bozas lives in Zululand and gives private art lessons. His paintings are shown in museums and art galleries around the world.

Bozas' paintings are realistic depictions of his surroundings and interests. He paints what he knows and understands.

In *Cane Cutting in Eshowe*, Bozas painted a landscape of the sugarcane fields that are abundant in Zululand, where he lives. He used deep rich colors to define the fields and soft blue tones for the sunny sky that washes over the South African landscape.

Bozas painted *Cane Cutting in Eshowe* in 1990. The painting measures 41" x 60" (103 x 142.2 cm). Bozas used oil on board to capture the rich sugarcane fields of Eshowe. South Africa is a leading producer of sugar. Sugarcane is a type of tall grass. The sweet juice from the stem of the sugarcane plant is made into sugar.

Map of South Africa

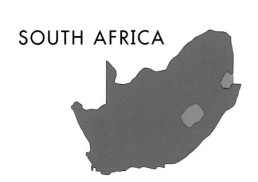

SOUTH AFRICA

Map of the continent of Africa

South Africa is located at the southern tip of the African continent. It is bordered in the west by the Atlantic Ocean and in the east by the Indian Ocean. South Africa has a varied landscape. The high, flat area in South Africa's interior is called the Central Plateau. The Kalahari Desert, north of the plateau, is known for its colorful red, brown, and white sand dunes. Surrounding the Central Plateau to the west, the south, and the east is the Great Escarpment, which is a chain of mountain ranges. Located on the eastern coast, the St. Lucia Wetlands are made up of lakes, swamps, dunes, and grasslands. They provide feeding grounds for many birds and animals, including pelicans and crocodiles.

14

1

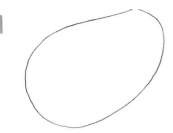

Start by drawing a large oval shape. Draw this shape lightly. It is a guide to help you draw South Africa. You will erase the shape in step 3.

2

Inside the oval shape draw the outline of South Africa. It will help if you first study the map of South Africa on the opposite page before you start to draw.

3

Erase the oval guide. Next we'll add some of South Africa's key places. For Table Mountain, draw two small vertical lines that are connected by a horizontal line. Add a circle on the upper right side for Johannesburg.

4

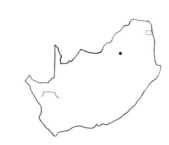

Draw a rectangle on the upper right side for Kruger National Park. You will learn more about this park on page 40.

5

Above the circle, draw a triangle. This is Sterkfontein Caves. You will read more about these famous caves on page 26. For Cape Town, draw a star.

6

⭐	Cape Town
•	Johannesburg
▭	Kruger National Park
△	Sterkfontein Caves
⌒	Table Mountain

If you like, draw the map key.
You are done!

The Flag of South Africa

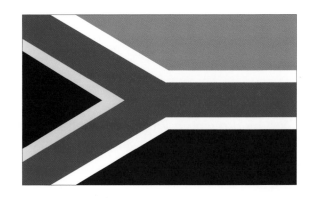

South Africa adopted its national flag in 1994. A government official named Fred Brownell designed the flag. He combined the colors from the nation's earlier flags. The flag of South Africa has a green horizontal Y shape, which symbolizes the unity of South African cultures. At the end of the Y shape on the left, there is a band of yellow that borders a black triangle. At the top of the flag is a red section, and at the bottom there is a blue section. Narrow bands of white separate these sections from the Y shape. There is no official symbolism for the flag's colors because the colors mean different things to different people. However, it is believed by many people that red represents the blood shed during Africa's history. Blue symbolizes the open sky, and green stands for the land. Black represents the black South Africans, and white stands for the white South Africans. Yellow symbolizes gold, one of the nation's most important resources.

1

Begin by drawing a large rectangle. Draw the rectangle big enough so that you can include all the sections of the flag.

2

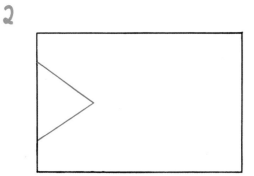

Draw a triangle shape on the left side of the rectangle.

3

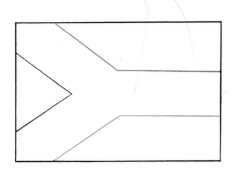

Draw the red lines shown above. After you are done, you will have a Y shape that is turned sideways. Good job!

4

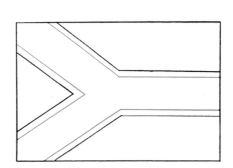

Within the Y shape you drew, draw a smaller Y shape.

5

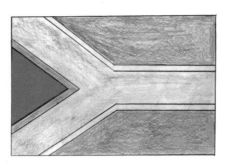

Finish by shading. You just drew the flag of South Africa.

17

The Blue Crane

The blue crane is the national bird of South Africa. This bird is found almost only on the open grasslands and plains of southern Africa. The blue crane is a long-legged bird that stands about 41 inches (104.1 cm) high. It has a long neck and strong front toes. The blue crane is named for the pale blue-gray feathers on its body and the long, dark blue feathers on its tail. It also has a fanlike crown of white feathers on its head.

The blue crane makes a loud call that sounds like "kraaarrk," and it dances to show joy. During this spectacular dance, the blue crane leaps high in the air, bows to other cranes, and stabs at sticks it has thrown up in the air. The blue crane feeds mostly on berries, seeds, insects, lizards, and mice.

1 To draw the blue crane, begin by drawing a curved shape as shown. This is your guide shape, so draw lightly.

2 Inside the guide shape, draw the outline of the blue crane. Notice how its head, thin neck, body, and tail are shaped. The bird is facing left.

3 Erase the guide shape. Add a rectangle under the bird's body. This is a guide to help you draw the crane's legs and feet.

4 Use the rectangle guide to draw the bird's legs and feet.

5 Erase the rectangle guide. Next add the blue crane's beak.

6 Erase the line between the beak and the head. On the blue crane's head, add the eye.

7 Shade the blue crane, and you are done. Notice where the shading is dark and where it is light.

The Springbok

The springbok is the national animal of South Africa. This small deerlike animal is 2 ½ feet (0.8 m) high and weighs about 88 pounds (39.9 kg). It has long ears and curved horns. The springbok was named for its odd manner of jumping, or springing, which is called pronking. The springbok jumps, or pronks, when it senses predators nearby, such as lions or cheetahs. To avoid being attacked by a predator, the springbok pronks 10 feet (3 m) up in the air while keeping its legs stiff and head lowered. When the springbok pronks several times in a row, it looks like a bouncing ball. The springbok also runs fast and can reach speeds of 50 miles per hour (80.5 km/h). The springbok likes dry, open grasslands, where it feeds on grass and leaves. During the summer, the largest herd of springbok is found in the Kalahari Desert.

20

1 Draw the guide shape as shown here. This will be the springbok's body.

2 Draw the three shapes as shown below. These are guides to help you draw the springbok's legs.

3 Draw the legs and feet. Notice that the rear leg extends in to the body. Add a square shape on top of its body. This is the outline to help you draw the head.

4 Erase the bottom rectangles. Use the square shape to outline the head and the springbok's long ears.

5 Erase the square guide shape. Add the two horns on top of the head. Draw four small horizontal lines on the springbok's legs to make hooves.

6 Draw horizontal lines inside the horn. Draw a *U* shape inside its face. Now add the eyes and details for the nose. Draw the curved lines on its body.

7 Finish the springbok by shading. Notice where the shading is dark and where it is light. Nice work.

21

The King Protea

The king protea was chosen as the national flower of South Africa in 1975. The king protea is a type of fynbos, which is Afrikaans for "fine bush." They are unique plants that grow in a small area on the Western Cape of South Africa. Fynbos is one of the world's six floral kingdoms. More than 5,000 kinds of fynbos do not grow anywhere else in the world other than South Africa. The king protea is one of the most spectacular plants of the fynbos group. The flower head of the protea can grow to be 12 inches (30.5 cm) across. Although the protea grows in several colors, the most popular is pink. The protea comes in many varieties. This is the reason botanist Carl von Linné named it for the Greek god Proteus. Proteus was known for changing his looks whenever he wished.

1

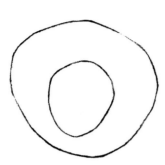

To draw the king protea, make two circles, one inside the other. These are guide shapes so make them light.

2

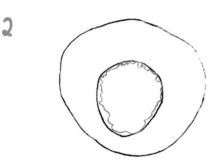

Inside the smaller circle, draw a ragged circle as shown. This line is the center of the flower.

3

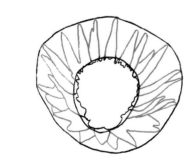

For the petals, draw pointed triangle shapes that fan out from the smaller circle. Notice that the petals do not go past the outer guide circle.

4

Erase the circle guides. Add leaves on the bottom left side of the flower.

5

Add a large leaf as shown. Inside the small circle, add another ragged circle.

6

Add the finishing details, and shade your king protea.

The Real Yellowwood Tree

South Africa's national tree is the real yellowwood. This tree was chosen because it has been growing in South Africa for more than 100 million years! From Cape Town in the southwest to the Drakensberg Mountains, the real yellowwood flourishes in the South African forests. This tree can reach 131 feet (39.9 m) in height. However, it does not grow to be very tall in open spaces. As the real yellowwood ages, its bark turns gray and peels off in strips. The real yellowwood produces cones that come in several colors, including white, pink, and light green. Early settlers in South Africa used the real yellowwood to build homes, furniture, and wagons. The real yellowwood is prized as one of South Africa's most beautiful native woods.

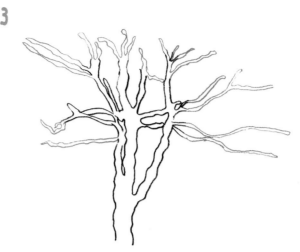

Start by drawing the trunk of the real yellowwood. Notice that there are three tree trunks. All three are shaped differently from one another.

Extend the branches even farther. Notice that the branches you are drawing in this step are long and thin. The more branches you draw, the fuller your tree will look. Be patient, and have fun drawing all the branches.

Add smaller branches that extend from the trunks that you drew in the last step. Notice that the branches get smaller toward the top.

To draw the leaves, shade all over the branches. Make sure you don't press down on your pencil too hard, or your shading will be too dark. You don't want to cover all the branches you worked hard to draw!

Prehistoric South Africa

South Africa is called the Cradle of Humankind because it is believed that modern man evolved from hominids that lived in the area millions of years ago. Hominids closely resemble modern man. Skeletons of the oldest hominids were discovered in the Sterkfontein Caves near Johannesburg. One hominid skeleton was named Little Foot. It is more than three million years old. Another skeleton was named Mrs. Ples, and it is two million years old. Fossils of plants and animals that existed during this time period were also found at Sterkfontein. Fossils are hardened remains of dead plants or animals that lived in prehistoric times.

Other findings at archaeological sites in South Africa include stone tools and bones that date from 110,000 years ago. They show how early people lived. Rock paintings 10,000 years old have been found throughout South Africa. These paintings show the lifestyle and religious beliefs of early humans.

1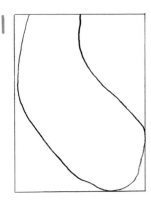
Begin by drawing a rectangle guide shape. Next draw the shape shown inside the rectangle. This will be the guide for the skeleton foot.

2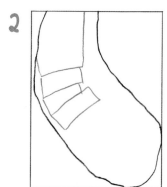
Draw the lines and rectangle shapes shown inside the foot guide shape. These shapes will help you to shape the bones in step 4.

3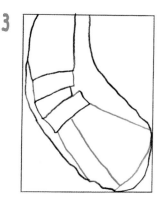
Draw three vertical lines and a curved horizontal line inside the foot guide shape. This is where you will draw the toe bones.

4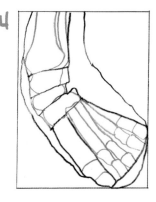
Using the photo, the red lines, and the guide shapes, start shaping the bones. Start from the ankle area and work your way down to the toes.

5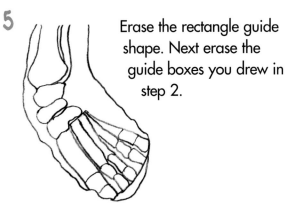
Erase the rectangle guide shape. Next erase the guide boxes you drew in step 2.

6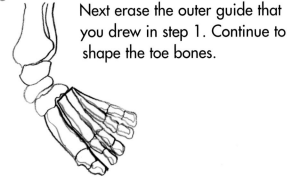
Next erase the outer guide that you drew in step 1. Continue to shape the toe bones.

7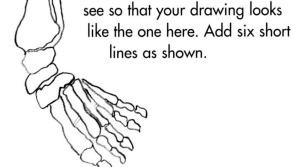
Next erase any extra lines you see so that your drawing looks like the one here. Add six short lines as shown.

8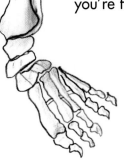
Shade the drawing, and you're finished.

Table Mountain

Cape Town is located on the Atlantic Ocean in southwestern South Africa. Towering over the city is Table Mountain, one of South Africa's most famous natural landmarks. The 3,563-foot (1,086-m) sandstone mountain looks like a table because it is flat on top. When clouds roll in, they drape over the mountain like a tablecloth! Table Mountain is part of a nature preserve that protects the plants and animals that live there. More than 1,470 different plant species exist on Table Mountain, which is about the same number of plant species that live in all of Great Britain! There is a cable car that takes people to the top of Table Mountain.

1

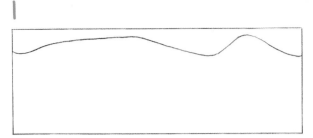

Start off with a large rectangle, and then draw a guideline at the top for the shape of the mountaintops.

2

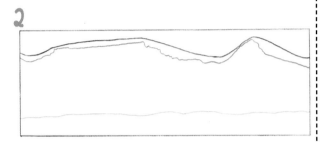

Inside the guideline, draw the shape of the mountaintops. The line is ragged in some areas and pointed in other areas. The straight part of the mountain is important. This is how Table Mountain earned its name. Now draw a guideline where the grass meets the bottom of the mountains.

3

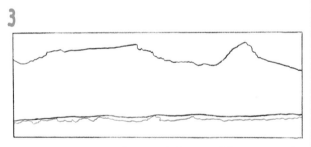

Erase the top guide, and then add a curved line to make the shape of the tree line at the bottom of the drawing.

4

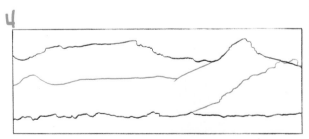

Erase the guideline, and start to add the shapes of the mountain slopes.

5

Draw in crooked lines for the shape of the mountain.

6

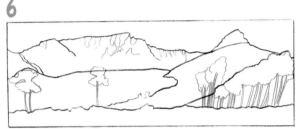

Add more lines to the mountains so that it looks rough and rocky. Start to draw the trees that line up at the bottom of the mountain.

7

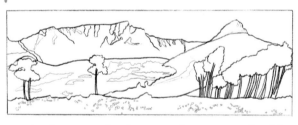

Finish drawing the lines to the mountain. Use curved shapes to add the details to the landscape.

8

Finish by shading your drawing. Make the valleys and the trees darkest.

Native South African Houses

The Ndebele, Zulu, and Xhosa peoples have homes that are indigenous to South Africa. The Ndebele home is made of mud blocks and is painted in bright colors. Ndebele women often make their own paints with natural materials. For instance white paint is made from lime, and brown colors are made from different soils. The Zulu house is round at the top, which makes it look like a beehive. Zulu men build the frame of the beehive house with tall sticks. Zulu women weave grass mats that are laid on the frame to cover it. Grass ropes are used to tie the mats to the frame. The Xhosa hut is made of mud mixed with cow dung. Its cone-shaped roof is thatched, which means it is covered with straw or grass.

1

You will draw a design of the pattern that brightly decorates a Ndebele house. Before you start, study the photograph on the opposite page. The design you will draw is highlighted. Begin by drawing a rectangle. Notice that the top and bottom lines continue past the end.

2

Add straight slanted lines to three of the corners as shown.

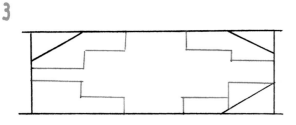

3

Draw the straight red lines as shown. It is easier if you draw one side at a time. Start at the top left side and work your way to the bottom. Now draw the right side.

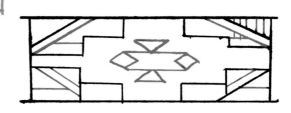

4

Draw the center shapes first. Notice the two triangles on the top and bottom and the two diamond shapes on the left and right. Now continue to add more straight lines near the corners. Some lines are horizontal and others are vertical. Draw one corner at a time.

5

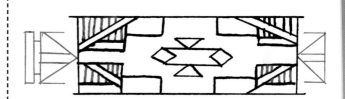

Draw vertical lines in the left top and bottom corners. Do the same on the lower right corner. You will now draw the shapes shown above on the outside of the rectangle you drew in step 1. Start on the left side and then draw the right side. Draw one shape at a time and take your time.

6

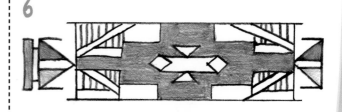

Finish by shading your drawing, and you are done.

31

The Castle of Good Hope

The oldest colonial building in South Africa is the Castle of Good Hope. It was built between 1666 and 1679, in the heart of Cape Town. The castle was built by the Dutch to defend their colony from invaders. The building is shaped like a pentagon, which means it has five sides. Its walls are 32 feet (9.8 m) high and almost 500 feet (152.4 m) long. A moat, or a deep ditch filled with water, surrounds the castle. At each of the five corners of the building, there is a bastion. A bastion is a fortified structure that sticks out from the main building to protect it during attacks. Inside the castle are apartments, called *kats*, where parties were held. Today the castle is a museum where visitors can see weapons and uniforms.

1

Begin drawing the Castle of Good Hope by drawing a large rectangle for a guide.

2

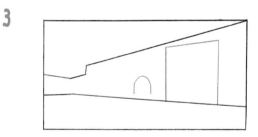

Draw the top line from left to right. Notice that the line slants upward to the right until it meets the upper right corner. The bottom line slants slightly downward.

3

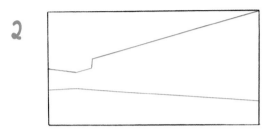

Inside the lines you drew in the last step, add a small arc for the window and a large square shape for the door.

4

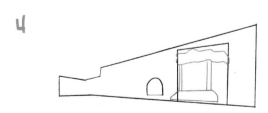

Erase the rectangle guide shape. Finish drawing the window. Next add the curved lines and columns inside the square. This will be the entrance.

5

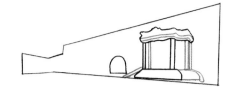

Erase the square guide shape of the door. Add more detail to the entrance by adding more lines to the columns and the base.

6

Next add the stairs to the entrance. Make a curved line inside the window. Finish this step by adding the bushes, shrubs, and roof and chimneys on the left.

7

Add different size rectangles throughout the drawing. These are windows. Notice how the sizes change.

8

Shade your castle, and you are done!

Shaka

Shaka was born in 1787 to a Zulu chief and a woman from another group. When he was about six years old, his mother and father separated. This forced Shaka and his mother to leave the Zulus. They went to live with the Mtetwa people. Shaka joined the Mtetwa army at age 21. He was a great warrior and became the army's highest leader. Shaka went to war against the Zulus and killed their tribal chief. Shaka soon became king of the Zulus. He introduced new battle tactics and a spear called the *assagai* spear. Under Shaka's rule the Zulus united many clans under the Zulu empire. When the British arrived in 1824, they gave Shaka gifts of blankets and jewelry. He in turn gave them some land. After Shaka died in 1828, the Zulus fought the Boers. In 1838, the Boers defeated the Zulus, ending their power in South Africa.

1

To draw Shaka, start with a small circle. Underneath the circle, draw a rounded rectangle shape.

4

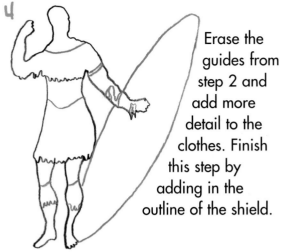

Erase the guides from step 2 and add more detail to the clothes. Finish this step by adding in the outline of the shield.

2

Shape Shaka's head and neck. Draw the guide shapes. First draw the square looking shape behind his head. Then draw the rectangle looking shape on the right. Draw his body guide shape. Notice this shape makes him look like he is wearing a long dress.

5

Continue to add detail to Shaka's clothing. Add the feather shape on top of his head. Now we are going to add the spear by drawing two straight lines and connecting them on the top and bottom as shown. Add the eyes, nose, mouth and chin to the face.

3

Erase the guides from step 1. Now add the details of the arms and legs. Note the clothing that Shaka is wearing and draw wavy lines to show detail.

6

Now you are ready to shade. Make the body and the spear dark. Add details to the shield. Lightly shade the clothes.

Blyde River Canyon

Blyde River Canyon runs parallel to the Great Escarpment in northeastern South Africa. The canyon is 2,297 feet (700.1 m) deep. The 15-mile (24.1-km) canyon is bordered on both sides by sheer cliffs and odd rock formations. One of the most interesting rock formations is called the Three Rondavels, because the sandstone towers look like round huts with thatched roofs. The Blyde River joins a river called the Treur River. Where the two rivers meet, water erosion has formed a magnificent geological feature called Bourke's Luck Potholes. The potholes are pools of water about 20 feet (6.1 m) deep. They were created by water spinning around the rock formations. The potholes were named for Tom Bourke, a prospector who searched for gold in the area.

1

To draw Blyde River Canyon, start with a large rectangle. This is a guide shape.

2

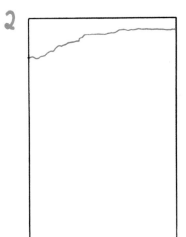

In the upper part of the rectangle, draw a ragged line. This will be the top of the canyon.

3

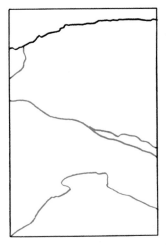

Add more lines for the many rocks and cliffs of the canyon. Study the red lines before you start to draw.

4

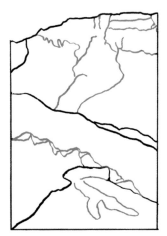

Erase the top part of the rectangle guide. Now add ragged and curved lines. Notice all the detail in the photograph before you start.

5

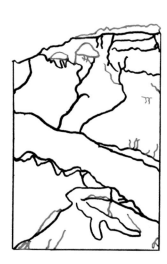

Add more detail to the canyon as shown in red.

6

Shade the canyon. Shade some areas darker than other areas to bring out the details of the many different kinds of rocks.

Fort Frederick

By the late 1700s, European Trekboers had moved to the eastern part of the Cape. They were farmers who searched for land on which to graze their cattle. They came into contact with the Xhosa herdsmen, who were also after rich grazing land. This started a century of frontier wars between the Trekboers and the Xhosa. Trekboers and other European settlers built frontier forts as protection from South Africans and other invaders. Built in Port Elizabeth in 1799, Fort Frederick was the first stone building on the Eastern Cape. The fort has a powder magazine that once held 2,000 pounds (907.1 kg) of gunpowder for the cannons. Today you can visit Fort Frederick and experience a part of South Africa's frontier history.

1

Let's start by drawing a large rectangle.

2

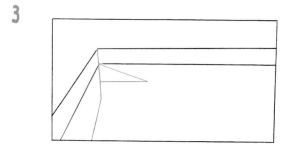

Draw the two lines as shown. The lines are next to one another. This is the wall.

3

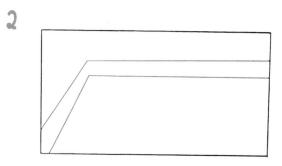

On the left corner, draw the line as shown above. Next add the triangle shape.

4

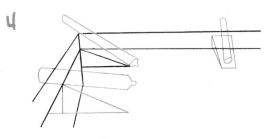

Add another triangle shape below the triangle you drew in step 3. Next draw the long tube shapes on top of the triangle shapes. These are cannons. Toward the right, draw a smaller cannon.

5

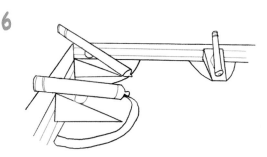

Erase the extra lines on the insides of the triangles and the cannons. Draw half circles around each of the cannons. They are the bases of the cannons.

6

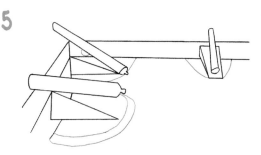

Add more detail to the drawing by adding circles and lines to the cannons to match the picture. Then add straight lines to the wall. This will help in the next step when the bricks are added.

7

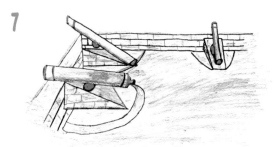

Draw straight lines for the bricks in the wall and in the triangle-shaped cannon platforms. After shading the drawing, you are done!

Kruger National Park

Kruger National Park is one of the oldest game preserves in the world and the biggest game park in South Africa. The park was named for former South African president Paul Kruger. In 1898, he wanted an area to preserve and protect the plants and the animals that lived there. Kruger National Park covers 7,523 square miles (19,484.5 sq km) and supports the greatest variety of wildlife species on the African continent. The park has 16 different ecosystems and 147 species of mammals. The most famous mammals include the lion, the leopard, the elephant, the buffalo, and the black rhinoceros, which you will learn how to draw. Hunters called these animals the Big Five, because they are the most dangerous. Today these animals are protected from hunters in this huge park. A rhino weighs about 1.2 tons (1100 kg) and is one of the largest land animals. It is almost 6 feet (1.8 m) high and about 15 feet (4.6 m) long.

1 Draw a circle. It doesn't have to be a perfectly round circle. This is a guide shape that will help you to draw the rhino's body.

2 Add the shape shown in red on the lower right side of the circle. This guide shape will help you to draw the rhino's head.

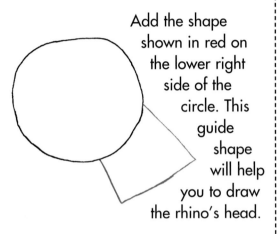

3 Inside the guide shapes, draw the outline for the rhino's face and body. Note the two horns on his head.

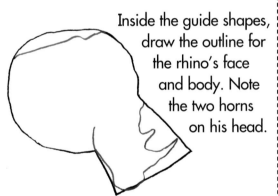

4 Erase the guide shapes. Draw the rhino's ear on the right side. At the bottom of the body, add two rectangles. These are guides to help you draw the legs.

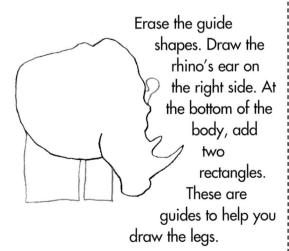

5 Next draw the shape of the rhino's legs inside the guide rectangles. Finish this step by adding an eye.

6 Erase the rectangle guides. Add curved shapes for the nose and upper leg and then some curved lines around the eyes to show wrinkles. Finish by adding an upside-down V shape for the other ear.

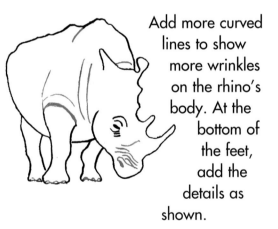

7 Add more curved lines to show more wrinkles on the rhino's body. At the bottom of the feet, add the details as shown.

8 After shading, you are done!

Robben Island

Robben Island, located near Cape Town, became famous during the apartheid era, when it served as a prison for people who protested against the government. One of the island's best-known prisoners was  Nelson Mandela. He was born in 1918 to the royal family of the Xhosa peoples. In 1964, Mandela was arrested for encouraging people to demonstrate against apartheid. He spent 26 years in prison, eighteen of those years were spent at Robben Island. In 1993, Mandela won the Nobel Peace Prize for his work in promoting democracy for his country. In 1994, Mandela became South Africa's first black president. Today the prison is a museum. It is also a memorial to the people who fought to make South Africa a democratic nation.

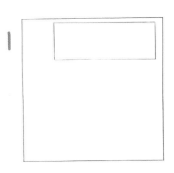

1 To draw Robben Island Prison, start by making a large square. Then draw a rectangle.

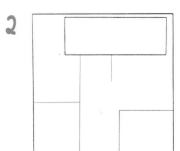

2 Draw the red lines, as shown. Study the lines and then draw one line at a time.

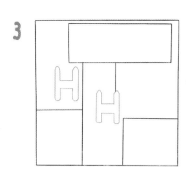

3 Start adding *H* shapes. Notice their placement. These shapes are different buildings.

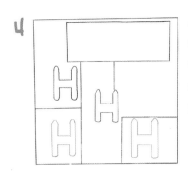

4 Add two more *H* shaped buildings, one on the left and one on the right.

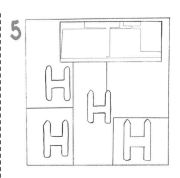

5 You will next add more buildings inside the rectangle you drew in step 1.

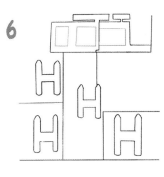

6 Erase the square and rectangle guides you drew in step 1. Draw smaller rectangle shapes as shown.

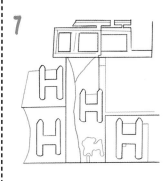

7 Continue drawing the lines for the building. Now you will add details such as streets and a bush.

8 You are now ready to shade. Shade some areas darker than others. Add as much detail as you like.

Timeline

1200	Bantu-speaking people move into southern South Africa.
1488	Cape of Good Hope is discovered by Portuguese sailors.
1498	Portuguese explorer Vasco da Gama sails around the Cape of Good Hope.
1652	The Dutch East India Company establishes a settlement at the Cape.
1820	British settlers arrive to farm the Eastern Cape.
1835	The Great Trek begins, the year the Boers move to the interior of South Africa
1867	Diamonds are found in South Africa.
1886	Gold is discovered near Johannesburg.
1899	The Anglo-Boer War begins.
1948	Apartheid is established as the national policy when the National Party comes to power.
1961	South Africa becomes independent of Britain.
1964	Nelson Mandela is sentenced to life in prison.
1990	President F. W. de Klerk frees Mandela from prison and ends apartheid.
1994	South Africa's first free elections are held, and Nelson Mandela is elected president.
1996	South Africa adopts a new constitution.

South Africa Fact List

Official Name	The Republic of South Africa
Area	471,445 square miles (1,221,036.9 sq km)
Population	43 million
Capital	Pretoria, Cape Town, and Bloemfontein
Most-Populated City	Johannesburg, population 5.7 million
Industries	Steel, processed food, chemicals, textiles
Agriculture	Corn, sugarcane, tobacco, wheat, cattle
Minerals	Gold, diamonds, coal, uranium
National Bird	Blue crane
National Flower	King protea
National Tree	Real yellowwood
National Animal	Springbok
National Fish	Galjoen
Longest River	Orange River, 1,300 miles (2,092.1 km)
National Holidays	Human Rights Day, March 21
	Freedom Day, April 27
	Day of Reconciliation, December 16
	Day of Goodwill, December 26
National Anthem	"The Call of South Africa"

Glossary

abundant (uh-BUN-dent) More than enough, plentiful.

ancestors (AN-ses-terz) Relatives who lived long ago.

archaeological (ar-kee-uh-LAH-jih-kul) Having to do with the study of the way humans lived long ago.

continent (KON-tin-ent) One of the seven great masses of land on Earth.

cultures (KUL-churz) The beliefs, practices, and arts of groups of people.

dangerous (DAYN-jer-us) Able to cause harm.

democratic (deh-muh-KRA-tik) In favor of democracy, a system in which people choose their leader.

demonstrations (deh-mun-STRAY-shunz) A public display or gathering for a person or a cause.

depictions (dih-PIKT-shunz) Images of something.

descendants (dih-SEN-dents) People born of a certain family or group.

designed (dih-ZYND) Planned the form of something.

develop (dih-VEH-lup) To grow.

dunes (DOONZ) Hills of sand piled up by the wind.

dung (DUNG) Animal waste.

ecosystems (EE-koh-sis-temz) Communities of living things and the surroundings, such as air, soil, and water, in which they live.

erosion (ih-ROH-zhun) The wearing away of land over time.

evolved (ee-VOLVD) Changed over many years.

floral (FLOR-ul) Of, relating to, or showing flowers.

fortified (FOR-tih-fyd) Made secure or strong.

frontier (frun-TEER) The edge of a settled country, where the wilderness begins.

geological (jee-uh-LAH-jih-kul) Relating to Earth's rocks and minerals.

graze (GRAYZ) To feed on grass.

indigenous (in-DIH-jeh-nus) Having started in and coming naturally from a certain area.

industries (IN-dus-treez) Moneymaking businesses in which many people work and make money producing a particular product.

interior (in-TEER-ee-ur) Inside.

invaders (in-VAYD-erz) People who enter a place in order to attack and conquer.

kingdoms (KING-dumz) The major divisions of living things.

mammals (MA-mulz) Warm-blooded animals that have a backbone and hair, breathe air, and feed milk to their young.

minority (my-NOR-ih-tee) The smaller part of a group or a whole.

parallel (PAR-uh-lel) Being the same distance apart at all points.

plateau (pla-TOH) A broad, flat, high piece of land.

policy (PAH-lih-see) A law that people use to help them make decisions.

predators (PREH-duh-terz) Animals that kill other animals for food.

prehistoric (pree-his-TOR-ik) The time before written history.

prime minister (PRYM MIH-nih-ster) The leader of a government.

republics (ree-PUB-liks) Forms of government in which the authority belongs to the people.

resources (REE-sors-ez) Supplies or sources of energy or useful materials.

rondavels (RON-duh-velz) Round farm homes with cone-shaped roofs made of grasses.

species (SPEE-sheez) A single kind of plant or animal.

spectacular (spek-TAK-yoo-lur) Very unusual and great.

symbolizes (SIM-buh-lyz-ez) Stands for something else.

textiles (TEK-stylz) Woven fabrics or cloths.

tortured (TOR-churd) Caused much pain.

unique (yoo-NEEK) One of a kind.

unity (YOO-nih-tee) Togetherness.

Index

Web Sites

Due to the changing nature of Internet links, PowerKids Press has developed an online list of Web sites related to the subject of this book. This site is updated regularly. Please use this link to access the list: www.powerkidslinks.com/kgdc/safrica/